HOW TO EARLY WITH CRYPTO CURRENCY

100x Gains In Cryptocurreny

Reuben Ademola

Table of Contents

INTRODUCTION

HOW TO RETIRE EARLY WITH CRYPTO CURRENCY

Cryptocurrency allows you take control, security and other benefit such as low taxed purchases, risk free, customers' obscurity, data or information probity. Freedom of payment represents the fact that cryptocurrency is the money of the future. Meanwhile, Crypto is based on cryptography.

Crypto is a digital currency and will soon be the currency of the future. They are mined using the internet.

Crypto depends on how well you manage your crypto and not the amount of crypto you own.

There are mining companies who sell coins to cover their expenses. Jobs can be ascertained in such companies. People resign from their jobs in other to concentrate on how to grow, expand and manage their crypto balance sheet which is crypto itself. Obtaining financial freedom can be inform of investing in crypto currencies like Bitcoin, Lite coins, Ethereum.

Retiring early, is something everyone wants at some point of their working life. And that's why cryptocurrency is here, to help change the world and to unban the access to be a part of the global economy and to help the low currency rate like Africa whose currency value is low.

Now here are steps you can take to retire early of cryptosystem;

CHAPTER 1

GETTING INTEREST

In other to be current, it's good to get all of Decentralized platform like Celsius network, crypto.com, nexo and blockfi. Holding crypto on Celsius wallet network is like buying stock and looking at the dividend that's what it feels like to get interest on crypto.

Putting your money or crypto to Celsius network, means your income is larger than your expenses in other to create more income. Getting paid in cell token over 12%EPR a year, can only be achieved by placing our assets in a stable coin. Let's take for instance you have a 100 thousand in your bank and you are getting as low as 0.01 for interest. Now, when you take that money and get it placed on a stable coin, you stand to get 10% interest. Keep in mind that every platform comes with their rate or kind of interest. You are capable of getting an average percentage with this Moreover, these rates are capable of increasing. Instead of just placing them on a stable coin you could place them on other platforms that increase rapidly alongside US dollar rate or value. Atimes it rises depending on the institutional money trending and also on demand.

As I told you earlier, crypto is going to keep expanding that's one of the reasons people invest in Bitcoin, cell token, Dash or any other token knowing that the rate increases alongside US dollar. Meanwhile, there is a need to acquire knowledge on compound interest.

CHAPTER 2

AFFILIATE MARKETING

There are people making 6 to 7 figures income because they have numerous people using and sharing their links. This simply means Referrals advertising through your link. Like have Binanace that pays 40% trading fees to any who refers and uses the link to trade on the platform. And there are other platform too like Celsius and coin base paying 20/20 to you and anyone else that uses their link. At your will, you can invest $100 crypto for a month and you rack up many $20 commission and its part of crypto.

Coin base, generates 10$ which is equivalent to situation when 100 people are using your link you get a 1000$ you could also advertise through YouTube videos, email list, paid marketing. When it comes to affiliate bills and using their advertising budgets into paying members to invite other people, crypto pays well. Affiliate blockfi members are complex and large. Same goes for Celsius. They have a lot of ways they pay members for referrals. Splitting your investment in all coins are called diversifying.

Having a lot of optional products for people to choose from involves having a lot of options to make a choice which is known as optionality

CHAPTER 3

SMASTER NODES

You are getting a coin to invest large in these master nodes that boosts' other operators to perform the main consensus functions of running a block chain and these needs lots of investors to invest, so basically, investments are needed. So in other words, master nodes requires much technical expertise. Through 7000 dash master nodes, you can get 6.05%. Getting master nodes are not easy to get with something. Mining activities are consumes most of the resources. To ensure that they provide genuine services as backbone to the block chain network, master nodes operate on collateral based system. And their operators are similarly financially rewarded as miners are when working on proof of work system. They are also known as bonded validator system

CHAPTER 4

MAKING SURE YOUR PORTFOLIO IS BALANCE

Make sure you have bitcoins and other top 10 Coins and getting decent percentage of your portfolio meanwhile, coins are less risky to put in like we have Bitcoins that was at a place where it could crash and has gotten to 12k for 3times in 3years, so a times things like this fluctuates. In other to keep it balanced, shouldn't get too many or too few investment project on.

CHAPTER 5

MAKE SURE YOUR WALLET IS SECURE

The reason why a lot of crypto are lost in vagrant transactions is that the traditional way of thinking is that if it's not your keys, then it's not your crypto. A Novices shouldn't consider placing your crypto on Coin base or Binance till there is a basic understanding of transacting in crypto. Then it is advisable to get a hard wallet which are LEDGER NANO S OR LEDGER NANO X. as I told you earlier, crypto worth nothing if they are not yours, so the hard wallet helps keep your wallet secure. The moment crypto rise, you cash out and have your financial freedom.

CHAPTER 6

DO NOT HODL, SELL AT THE TOP

Each time you earn brownies from strangers on the internet, remember that to see your future, you need to see your past and learn from it. Now, the points you got are not worth your net worth

Instead when you earn points from brownies, the value of your net worth depreciates. At that point you are advised to cash out using the crypto.com.

CHAPTER 7

PASSIVE INCOME

We should work on producing a passive income from investments. There are principles that you can use whenever you want to do it with stocks market, Real estate bonds and many more, and not on people who aren't able to realize much money from cryptocurrency because they need to get a passive income to cover their expenses. People have believed so much in this idea that "they are going to get crypto cheap (lower or at its lowest rate) and then when it rises, "they will sell it and leave the market and venture into stocks." Problems with this strategy are;

Massive tax involves Putting your crypto in ethereum that will generate passive income with the money rather than selling your crypto with large money and when you invest you will be payed a tax. In other words choose the path that will be more convenient to go through.

Smart contract is a kind of currency that allows some collectible barg that would create opportunities through assets for people to apply and add value to peoples' life which is powered by Fungible and Non fungible tokens to stake on it.

CHAPTER 8

LONG TERM STRATEGY

This requires you keeping part of your investment for a long period of time cam also be seen as long term Investment. The prices get volatile from 5%to 10% as the market gets' bigger. A times, people choose to Defi-Because there are many risk with smart contract and there is a high rate of unstable profit of return meanwhile, in staking strategy, the only thing you get to witness or take note of is the graph AKA Staking Graph.

CHAPTER 9

FUNDAMENTAL SKILL IN BLOCK CHAIN

You can only be your own boss and have others work under you, when you acquire skills from Block chain which comes with huge opportunities like getting employed by a block chain company and earn 300,000 bucks yearly. Getting such opportunity requires hard work and focus. Acquiring skills like block chain developer and having a knowledge about technical operations while investing, makes you outstanding in the market. Investing a part of your earnings in one of those crypto platform like bitcoin is a good idea. Makes it easier to balance your portfolio and gives you more insights on creating your own block chain technology. It also gives you eligibility in getting involved in some community block chain that also builds your knowledge on crypto investment. Still on the quest to being own boss.

Getting more coins means reinvesting your crypto in different places in coins where you get returns in big figures and when the price goes high, you can still sell from it (optional)

Note: Investing too much can create unnecessary anxiety and fear of loss.

Which can make you sell quickly and make regrettable hasty decisions because of fear of loss.